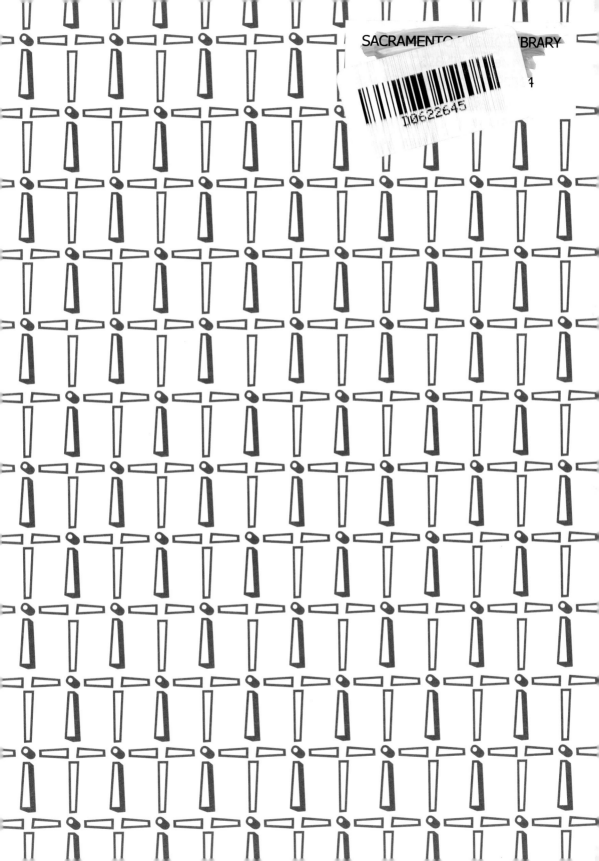

Jonah and the Big Fish

AND OTHER BIBLE STORIES

BY REBECCA GLASER

ILLUSTRATED BY BILL FERENC AND EMMA TRITHART

SPARK HOUSE FAMILY

MINNEAPOLIS

Contents

24 23 22 21 20 19 18 17 16 15   1 2 3 4 5 6 7 8
ISBN: 978-1-4514-9997-1

Book design by Toolbox Studios, Dave Wheeler, Alisha Lofgren, and Janelle Markgren
Illustrations by Bill Ferenc and Emma Trithart

Library of Congress Cataloging-in-Publication Data

Glaser, Rebecca Stromstad, author.
   Jonah and the big fish and other Bible stories / by Rebecca Glaser ; illustrated by Bill Ferenc and Emma Trithart.
        pages cm. — (Holy Moly Bible storybooks)
   Summary: «Illustrated retellings of the story of Jonah and the Big Fish and other favorite Bible stories."— Provided by publisher.
   Audience: Ages 5–8
   Audience: K to grade 3
   ISBN 978-1-4514-9997-1 (alk. paper)
1. Jonah (Biblical prophet)—Juvenile literature. 2. Samuel (Biblical judge)—Juvenile literature. 3. David, King of Israel—Juvenile literature. 4. Daniel (Biblical figure)—Juvenile literature. 5. Bible stories, English—Old Testament. I. Ferenc, Bill, illustrator. II. Trithart, Emma, illustrator. III. Title.
   BS580.J55G53 2015
   221.9ʹ505—dc23
                              2015012807

Printed on acid-free paper

Printed in U.S.A.

V63474; 9781451499971; AUG2015

God Calls Samuel

Samuel was a boy who lived in the temple with an old priest named Eli. He served Eli, helping him with whatever he needed. One night, when Samuel was sleeping, he heard a voice calling.

(Saaamuuuelll!)

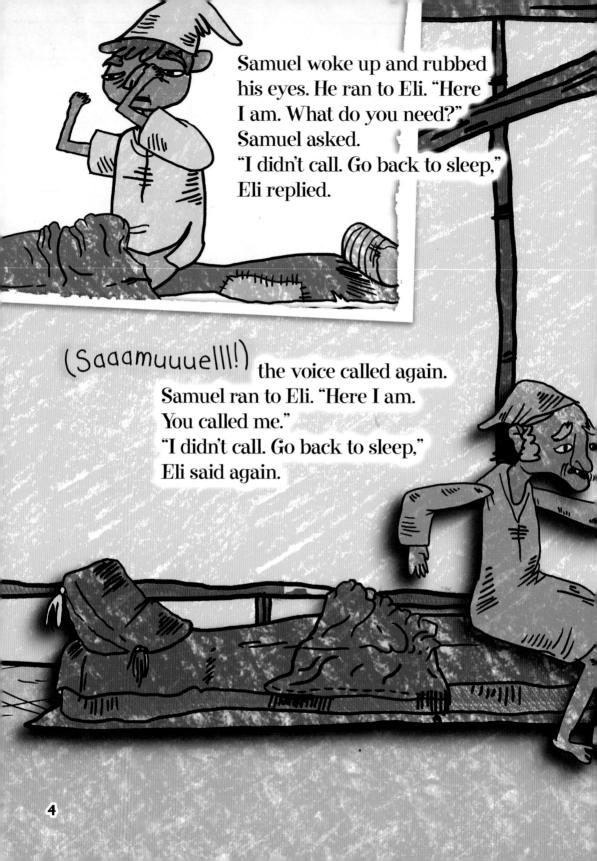

Samuel woke up and rubbed his eyes. He ran to Eli. "Here I am. What do you need?" Samuel asked.
"I didn't call. Go back to sleep," Eli replied.

(Saaamuuuelll!) the voice called again.
Samuel ran to Eli. "Here I am. You called me."
"I didn't call. Go back to sleep," Eli said again.

(Saaamuuuelll!) the voice called a third time. Samuel ran to Eli. This time, Eli realized it was God calling. He told Samuel, "Next time say, 'Speak, Lord. Your servant is listening.'"

Samuel Anoints David

God spoke to the prophet Samuel:
"It's time to choose a new king! Fill your horn with oil and go to the family of Jesse. I'll show you who will become the next king of Israel."

Samuel set off to meet Jesse's family and find the new king. When he arrived, he was amazed by Jesse's sons.

Some were big and strong. Others were skilled and smart. Samuel was sure one of these would be the new king.

Thump, thump, thump, thump. Jesse's oldest, biggest son stepped forward. Surely he would make a good king!

The other sons laughed.
"Ha! David's not fit to
 be king!"
"He's too young!"
"He's too small!"
"He's too stinky!"
But Samuel sent them to
fetch David.

Draw what you
think a king
looks like.

When young David stepped forward,
God spoke to Samuel:
"This is the one. David
will be the next king of Israel."
Samuel anointed David. He took some
oil from his horn and put it on David's
head. From that day, God's Spirit
stayed with David.

Color in
David to
show that h
received th
Spirit of Go

David and Goliath

hile David was caring for his sheep, e Israelites were battling the hilistines. In front of the Philistine my stood a mighty **BIG** man named oliath. **"Who will fight me?"** oliath shouted.

Goliath was HUGE! His legs were as big as trees! The Israelites were afraid. No soldier dared fight the giant—not even King Saul.

"I'll do it," David said. The soldiers and King Saul couldn't believe it. How could little David fight **HUGE** Goliath?

King Saul gave David heavy metal armor to wear and a big, sharp sword to fight with. But David realized, "I'm not going to win this fight with a sword! God will protect me!"

David shook off the heavy armor and picked up his sling and five smooth stones.

Goliath laughed. **"Do you think you can defeat me with five little stones?"** he roared.

"I can with God's help," David called back. He ran toward Goliath, loaded his sling, and launched the stone at his enemy.

THWAP!

The stone hit Goliath right in the forehead. **THUD!**

Goliath fell to the ground. David had defeated Goliath! The Philistine army ran awa

HOORAY!

With God's help, young David was a hero!

Daniel and the Lions

Of all the advisors who worked for King Darius, Daniel was the king's favorite. Daniel was an excellent advisor. He was honest, and the king trusted him.

The king's other advisors were jealous. They wanted Daniel to get in trouble, but Daniel never broke any laws. The advisors decided to trick the king into making a new law.

Draw yourself praying to God.

The new law said that EVERYONE had to worship the king. If ANYONE prayed to someone else, they would be thrown into the lions' den.

Daniel worshipped and prayed to ONLY God. The king's advisors knew that Daniel would break the new law.

One day, the advisors caught Daniel praying to God. "GOTCHA!" they shouted. They grabbed him and took him to the lions' den. Even the king couldn't save Daniel!

Daniel tumbled into the pit. A large stone covered the hole so Daniel couldn't escape. He closed his eyes and prayed.

"I worship God, and only God, not kings, not queens—no others on earth," Daniel prayed.

King Darius worried about Daniel all night. In the morning, he hurried to the lions' den."Has your God rescued you?" the king called down to Daniel.

"I'm safe!" Daniel shouted up to the king. "God sent an angel, who shut the lions' mouths."

Daniel climbed out of the pit. "The lions didn't hurt me because God protected me," he said. "I worship God, and only God, not kings, not queens—no others on earth."

King Darius jumped for joy! He made a new law telling everyone to worship Daniel's God.

Color King Darius.

Jonah and the Big Fish

Jonah was God's prophet. God told him,

"Go to Nineveh! I need you to deliver a message to the people there."

Jonah did NOT want to go. "Who, me? No way! I won't go there!" he said.

Without another word, Jonah ran away. He climbed on a ship and sailed far from Nineveh. God sent a BIG storm that battered the ship.

The worried sailors threw off some cargo and tried to row back to shore. Nothing worked

Color the fish God sent to swallow Jonah.

The crew pushed Jonah off the ship. SPLASH! Jonah landed in the sea. Right away the storm stopped.

GULP! God sent a large fish to swallow Jonah.

For three days, Jonah waited inside the stinky belly of the fish. He prayed, "God, please get me out of here! I promise to go to Nineveh!"

29

God heard Jonah's prayer and made the fish spit him out on the beach. "Thank you, God!" Jonah cheered.

Again, God told Jonah, **"Go to Nineveh!"** Jonah faced his fear and followed God's command. He brought God's message to Nineveh.

More Activities

LOOK AND FIND

Find the word *Lord* in the God Calls Samuel story on pages 3–6.

Lord is another name we use for God. Samuel and Eli would also have referred to God as *Yahweh* (YAH-way), which means "I am."

Find the

in the Samuel Anoints David story on pages 7–12.

Samuel anointed David with oil. Anointing a king was like crowning him, and in Israel a crown wasn't used.

Find the

in the David and Goliath story on pages 13–18.

As a boy, David was a shepherd who cared for his sheep. As an adult, David was a king who cared for God's people.

Find the

in the Daniel and the Lions story on pages 19–24.

In Daniel's time, lions were hunted and trapped in pits. These pits are also called dens.

Find the word *Nineveh* in the Jonah and the Big Fish story on pages 25–30.

It is pronounced "NIH-neh-vuh." Nineveh was one of the oldest and greatest ancient cities until its destruction in 612 BC. It was located along the Tigris River near what is today Mosul, Iraq.

ACTION PRAYER

Dear God, *(press palms together)*

Sometimes the world seems big, sooo big, *(open arms wide)*

And we feel small, sooo small, *(move palms closer together)*

But whether our troubles are big, sooo big, *(open arms wide)*

Or small, sooo small, *(move palms closer together)*

We trust that you can handle them all! *(lift hands high)*

Amen.

MATCHING GAME

Match the person from the Bible with the fact about them.

1.
Samuel lived in the temple with me when he was a boy.

2.
God chose me to be a king of Israel. My name means "beloved."

3.
I was protected by an angel sent by God to shut the lions' mouths.

4.
God called me to be a prophet. I anointed the first two kings of Israel.

5.
I was almost ten feet tall, but it only took one small stone to stop me.

6.
God called me to go to Nineveh. My name means "dove, the son of truth."

7.
I had seven sons and began a family line of kings that led to Jesus.